On sun-soaked stone and dark cave walls,
from the rocky deserts of the United States . . .

to the lush rainforests of Indonesia . . .

time capsules wait to be rediscovered.

These treasures teem with colorful stories about our past. Through them, we are transported and can find our place in the . . .

ANCESTORY

HANNAH SALYER

CLARION BOOKS

An Imprint of HarperCollinsPublishers

These time capsules take the shape of ancient rock paintings, drawings, and etchings.

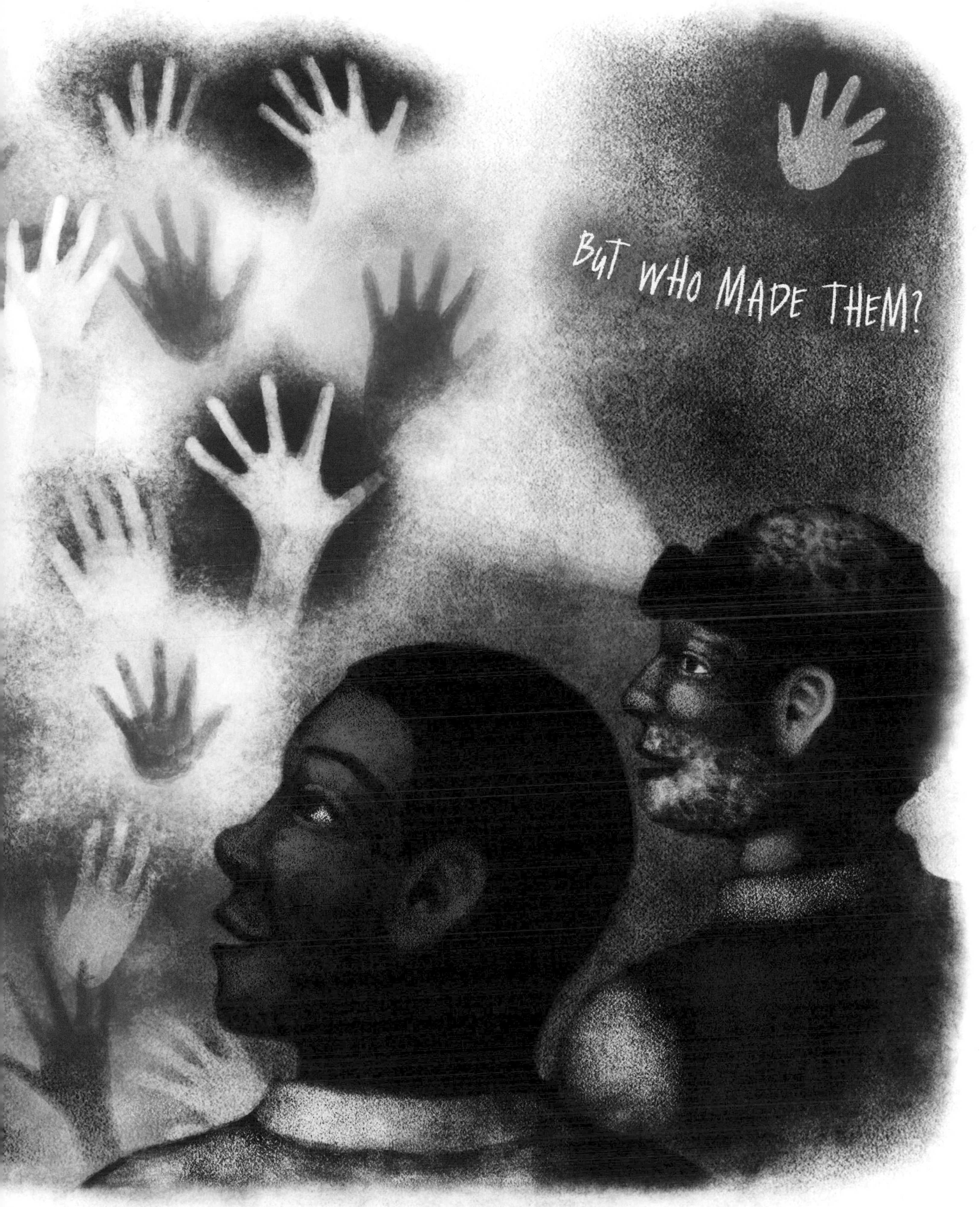
BUT WHO MADE THEM?

OUR ANCESTORS.

Homo sapiens, our own species. Neanderthals too.
Their art can be found all over the world.

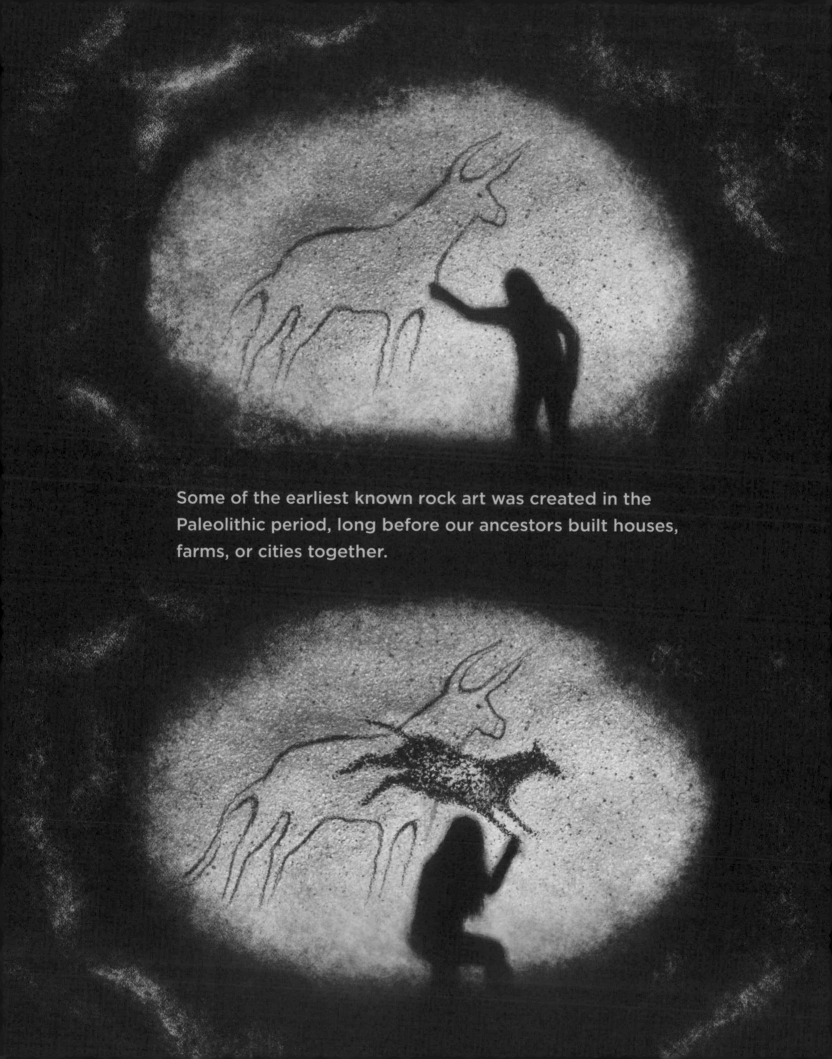

Some of the earliest known rock art was created in the Paleolithic period, long before our ancestors built houses, farms, or cities together.

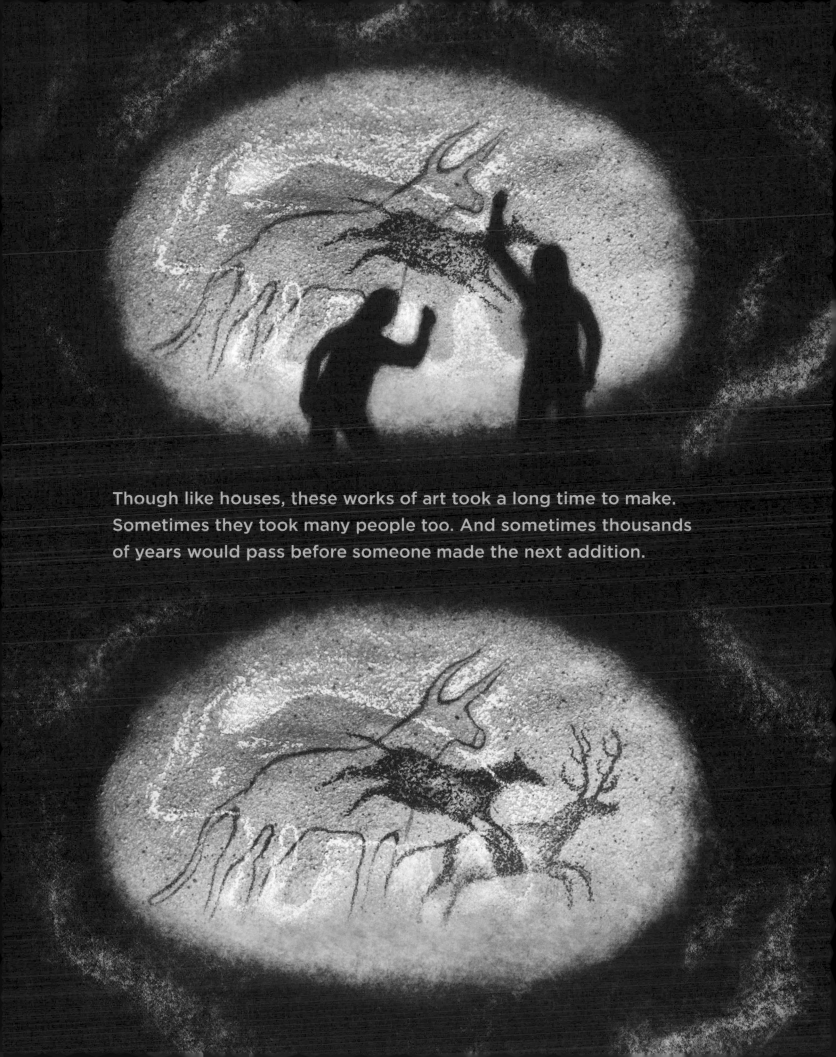

Though like houses, these works of art took a long time to make. Sometimes they took many people too. And sometimes thousands of years would pass before someone made the next addition.

EACH HANDPRINT, MARKING, COLOR, AND MATERIAL HAD A PURPOSE.

IT TOOK AN ENORMOUS EFFORT TO MAKE EACH PIECE.

Our ancestors did not have paint or brushes or pencils or ink.
They had to rely on minerals from their surroundings instead.

IRON OXIDE

MALACHITE

CALCITE

LIMONITE

YELLOW OCHRE

RED HEMATITE

AZURITE

GOETHITE

CHARGOAL

MANGANESE

ASH

CUPRITE

CARVED PICK

FLINT

YUCCA STALK

SHELL

SELENITE

They had to create their own handmade tools to etch into and draw on the stone.

Some of the markings and creatures shown in the art are symbols. These pictures represent something real or imagined and can work together to tell a longer story, like letters in an alphabet.

Mataral, Bolivia
Approximately 5,000–9,000 years old

Drakensberg Mountains, South Africa
Approximately 3,500 years old

Ushakothi, India
Approximately 800–2,000 years old

Najran, Saudi Arabia
Approximately 10,000–17,000 years old

Kimberley, Australia
Approximately 10,000–17,000 years old

Twyfelfontein (Ui-//aes), Namibia
Approximately 5,000 years old

Cantabria, Spain
Approximately 64,000 years old

Oregon, United States
Approximately 300–500 years old

Kirkkonummi, Finland
Approximately 3,500–5,000 years old

THERE ARE ALSO NUMEROUS ANIMALS SHOWN IN THESE PIECES WHO ARE NOW LONG EXTINCT.

IRISH ELK
Megaloceros
alive until approx.
8,000 years ago

MOA
Dinornis robustus
alive until approx.
600 years ago

AUROCHS
Bos primigenius primigenius
alive until approx.
400 years ago

EURASIAN WILD HORSE
Equus ferus ferus
alive until approx.
120 years ago

WOOLLY RHINO
Coelodonta antiquitatis
alive until approx.
9,000 years ago

WOOLLY MAMMOTH
Mammuthus primigenius
alive until approx.
11,700 years ago

EURASIAN CAVE LION
Panthera spelaea
alive until approx.
13,000 years ago

CAVE BEAR
Ursus spelaeus
alive until approx.
24,000 years ago

The lives of our ancestors were filled with difficulties and danger.
They worked hard to survive.
And yet, for thousands of years and despite their struggles . . .

THEY TOOK THE TIME TO CREATE.

The planet has changed in countless ways since these works were made.
Oceans and ice caps have expanded and then disappeared.

What was once green and blue has turned dry and dusty.

However, these ancient artworks remain—distant memories in stone of what came before us.

Some have been preserved in caves.
Others have weathered the elements outdoors.

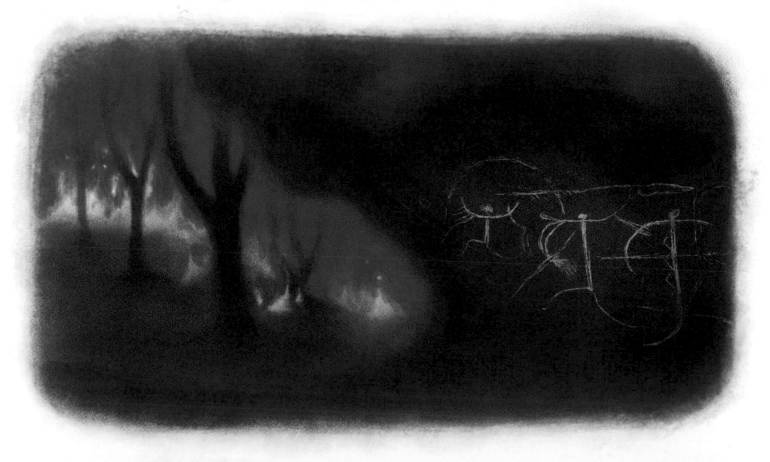

Today they are incredibly fragile and can be lost in the blink of an eye if we are not careful to protect them.

When it gets dark, these pictures reveal more of their secrets and their power. They come alive in light and shadow.

Our ancestors used natural shapes in the stone to help define the creatures, so that they seem to emerge from the walls. They were drawn by the light of the setting sun or a flickering flame.

IN THOSE GLIMMERS, THE FIGURES DANCE, LEAP, AND RUN.

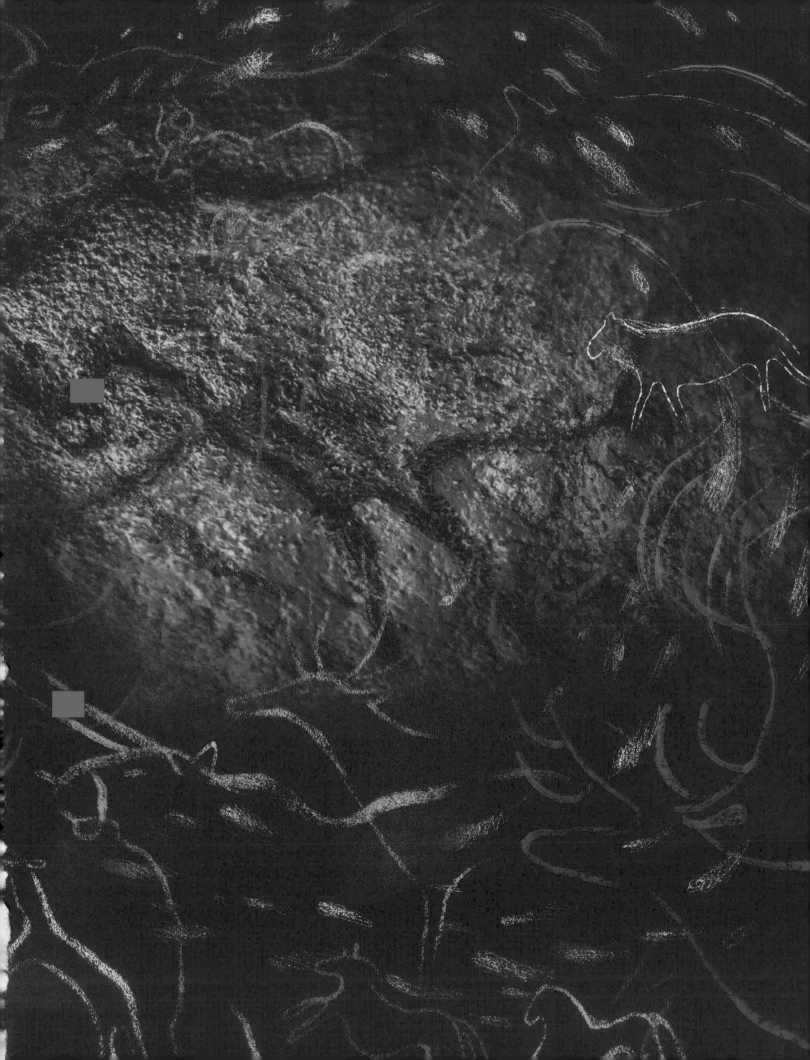

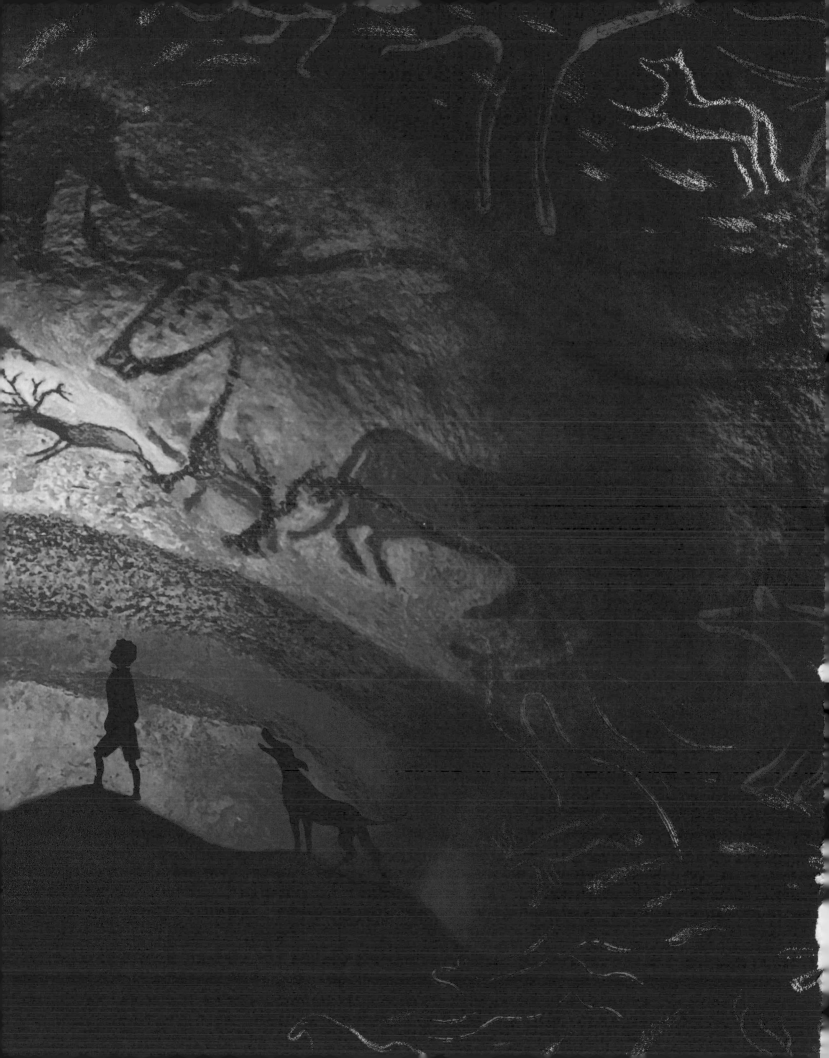

Many of the sites also have unique soundscapes:
Deep, resonant chambers, rocks that ring when
they are hit, and walls that seem to talk back.

WHAT DID OUR ANCESTORS THINK WHEN THEY HEARD THESE ECHOES?

COULD THE ART THEY MADE BE MAPPING THE STARS?
DOCUMENTING THE WORLD AROUND THEM?

Were the sites gateways to connect with spaces
and spirits invisible to the naked eye?

We don't have every clue that we need to know exactly why our ancestors created these pictures or the details of the stories they were telling. Through hard work, though, bits of evidence continue to be found. Archaeologists study tirelessly to connect the dots, and sometimes people who are part of local indigenous communities still have distant familiarity with these ancient sites and stories.

One thing is clear: The locations where our ancestors made their art were very important.

They are still important to us because these places hold pieces of our history on the planet. They are our human heritage.

If we step back, these fragments reveal a picture of a larger, ongoing story.

The outlines of this shared story are old,
but they are still being drawn. Even now,
the story is unfurling all around you.

SITE MAP

Not every single rock art site is listed here, and new ones are always being rediscovered!

NORTH AMERICA

Alberta, Canada—Áísínai'pi (Writing-on-Stone) Provincial Park petroglyphs
Alberta, Canada—Zephyr Creek, Highwood Provincial Recreation Area pictographs
British Columbia, Canada—Petroglyph Provincial Park, Nanaimo
Nunavik Region (Northern Quebec), Canada—Qajartalik carvings
Ontario, Canada—Anishinaabe Rock Paintings of Agawa Rock
Alaska, United States—Rock shelters of Tuxedni Bay and Clam Cove
California, United States—Coso Region petroglyphs
Georgia, United States—Track Rock Gap Petroglyph Site
Hawaii, United States—Puakō Petroglyph Park
Montana, United States—Bear Gulch pictographs
Nevada, United States—Grapevine Canyon petroglyphs
Tennessee, United States—Rock art of the Cumberland Plateau
Texas, United States—White Shaman mural
Utah, United States—Horseshoe Canyon petroglyphs
Washington, United States—Columbia River Gorge petroglyphs

CENTRAL AMERICA & CARIBBEAN ISLANDS

Dominican Republic—Pomier Caves rock art
Mexico—Rock art of Tamaulipas Mountains
Mexico—Sierra de San Francisco murals
Mexico—La Pila Del Rey petroglyphs
Puerto Rico—Rock art of Mona Island caves
US Virgin Islands—Reef Bay Trail petroglyphs

SOUTH AMERICA

Argentina—Cueva de los Manos rock art
Chile—Taira Valley rock art
Colombia—Rock art of Guaviare región, Cerro Azul Hill
Bolívia—Camargo, Chuquisaca, rock art
Brazil—Serra da Capivara National Park paintings
Brazil—Ilha de Santa Catarina rock art
Peru—Checta petroglyphs
Venezuela—Amazonas, Atures Rapids petroglyphs

EUROPE

Britain—Northumberland rock art carvings
Finland—Kirkkonummi rock art
France—Cosquer cave paintings
France—Chauvet Cave paintings
France—Font-de-Gaume rock art
France—Lascaux Caves paintings
France—Pech Merle Cave paintings
Italy—Valcamonica petroglyphs
Norway—Rock art of Alta
Spain—Altamira Cave paintings
Spain—La Pasiega Cave paintings

AFRICA

Algeria—Rock art of Tassili n'Ajjer

Gabon—Lope-Okanda National Park petroglyphs

Libya—Tadrart Acacus rock art

Madagascar—Andriamamelo Cave rock art

Mali—Bandiagara Cliffs rock art

Mauritania—Oued Jrid (Jrid Wadi) pictographs

Morocco—Gravures rupestres d'Ait Ouazik

Namibia—Twyfelfontein (/Ui-//aes) rock art carvings

Niger—Dabous giraffe petroglyphs

South Africa—Pictographs of the San people

South Africa—Blombos Cave rock art carvings

Sudan—Gabal El Uweinat rock art

Zimbabwe—Matobo Hills rock art

ASIA

China—Huashan rock art

China—Petroglyphs of the Helan Mountains

India—Ushakothi cave paintings

Indonesia—Sulawesi rock art

Iran—Yāfte Cave rock art

Korea—Bangudae Petroglyphs, Daegok-ri, Ulju artifacts

Mongolia—Tsagaan Salaa rock art

Nepal—Kya Valley, Mustang, cave paintings

Pakistan—Swat Valley rock art

Russia—Khasaut Gorge cave paintings

Saudi Arabia—Najran petroglyphs

Sri Lanka—Hulannuge rock art

Thailand—Sam Roi Yot National Park cave paintings

AUSTRALIA & PACIFIC ISLANDS

Fiji—Vatulele Island rock art

New Zealand—Takiroa Rock Art Shelter

Papua New Guinea—Karawari Caves rock art

Tonga—Foa Island petroglyphs

New South Wales, Australia—Ku-ring-gai Chase National Park rock art

Northern Territory, Australia—Kakadu National Park rock art

Queensland, Australia—Quinkan Country rock art

Tasmania, Australia—Preminghana petroglyphs

Victoria, Australia—Grampians National Park rock art

Western Australia—Burrup Peninsula, Pilbara, rock art

Western Australia—Kimberley Region rock art

A STORY WITHIN A STORY:
THE REDISCOVERY OF THE LASCAUX CAVES

On September 8, 1940, much of the world was at war. In the south of France, a boy named Marcel Ravidat brought his dog, Robot, and his friends Jacques Marsal, Georges Agnel, and Simon Coencas back to an opening in the ground that Robot had fallen in while chasing a rabbit. The boys had been on the lookout for rumored treasure and secret tunnels leading to a nearby mansion—could this be it?

Little did they know that what they were about to find would profoundly impact the field of archaeology, art, and human history. At the end of their descent into the cavern, they held up their lanterns to reveal a breathtaking constellation of painted fauna all around them. With every shift of a lantern, the animals seemed to move.

More than 600 paintings cover the walls inside the Lascaux Caves. After much doubt as to the authenticity of the paintings, it was determined by prehistorians that the art was legitimate. The caves were then opened to the public, and over the next two decades, thousands of people got to see the artwork for themselves. During this time, the breath of the visitors drastically changed the composition of the atmosphere, and condensation formed on the walls and ceilings. Moisture sullied the paintings. Mold developed. High-powered lighting caused the paintings to fade. They had been irrevocably damaged by their popularity.

Lascaux was finally closed to the public in 1963, and since then only experts are allowed to enter at very limited capacity. The site was designated as a UNESCO world heritage site in 1979. A replica of the site was built nearby in 1983 and draws 300,000 visitors a year. Today, dating estimates that the Lascaux paintings were created by different people over a period of time approximately 17,000 years ago. Much debate continues over various aspects of the Lascaux Caves, but it remains an iconic visual reflection of our ancestors and our past.

Author's Note

By the time you read this book, even more new information about rock art has probably come to light. Because rock art exists in "deep time," there is still so much to uncover. In Rebecca Wragg Sykes's book, *Kindred: Neanderthal Life, Love, Death and Art,* she offers up a trick to help us understand the timescale of our species and the planet. Thinking of the universe's 13.8 billion years as if it were a single 12-month calendar "puts the dinosaurs shockingly close to Christmas, while the earliest *Homo sapiens* arrive only a few minutes before New Year's fireworks." We have roughly only 3 percent of modern human history recorded in writing. But writing is not the only remnant that can hold history. Rock art is special because it is a recorded past that goes back *much* further. Rock art gives us unique insight into the lives, dreams, and stories of our ancient ancestors.

It's important to recognize, though, that to our ancestors making these magnificent markings, it was not merely art. The term "rock art" is actually a *misnomer* (a wrong name or designation). To our ancestors, the works were functional, held information, and in many ways were considered to contain connections to spirits, energies, and planes of existence. They can continue to hold that importance for us, in addition to being significant time capsules.

Right now, those same time capsules are at risk of being lost due to climate change (extreme weather can alter the conditions that allowed the art to survive for so long) and land development. Sadly, there are also rock art sites that continue to be vandalized by people who don't understand that these works are a unique human heritage. If ever you should happen upon a rock art site, it's important to look but not touch! Oils in our hands can contribute to deterioration of the markings. You can help protect sites by reaching out to the local park system, land management, or historical society, who can assist with the safekeeping and documentation of the site. You can also support and uplift local indigenous communities, who hold the threads of many ancient cultures and stories that connect us to the past. We must work together to preserve these early chapters in our ANCESTORY.

Hannah visits the great gallery in Horseshoe Canyon, UT.
Photo by Ester Kwon

WORDS TO KNOW

ACOUSTICS: A branch of physics that deals with the study of "mechanical waves" or movements in gasses, liquids, and solids. It covers areas such as vibration, sound, ultrasound (higher than humans can hear), and infrasound (lower than humans can hear).

ARCHAEOLOGY: The study of human activity through the collection and analysis of artifacts. Archaeologists draw evidence from biological, geological, and environmental systems in their study of the past. The archaeological record consists of artifacts, architecture, organic material, and development of culture through human interaction with the environment.

CARBON DATING: A process that measures the decay of a certain type of atom found in a once-living organism to determine when it was last alive. This method works by analyzing the characteristics of Carbon-14, a radioactive version of carbon atoms that naturally occur in the atmosphere.

HOMO SAPIENS: The most widespread species of primate, designated by ability to walk on two legs (bipedality), having large, complex brains that enable the advancement of sophisticated tools, culture, and language.

INDIGENOUS: Originating or occurring naturally in a particular place; native.

MESOLITHIC ERA: A period in human prehistory, following the Paleolithic era, connected to the decline in the group hunting of large animals. People began to prefer a hunter-gatherer way of life, and with it came the development of more refined stone tools and weapons than those created during the Paleolithic.

NEANDERTHAL: An extinct species of ancient humans who lived in Eurasia until about 40,000 years ago.

NEOLITHIC ERA: A period in human prehistory, following the Mesolithic, that shifted the way people behaved in communities, and the culture that was created as a result of these changes. The biggest shift was the introduction of farming and domestication of certain animal species.

PALEOLITHIC ERA: A period in human prehistory marked by the invention of stone tools that covers a large period (roughly 99 percent) of human technological prehistory. It extends from the earliest known use of stone tools by hominids, around 3.3 million years ago, to the end of the Pleistocene.

PARIETAL ART: Markings made by humans on vertical stone surfaces. Much of the surviving historic and prehistoric rock art is found on cave walls or in partly enclosed rock shelters; this may also be termed "cave art" or "rock art."

PETROGLYPH: An image created by removing part of a rock surface by incising, picking, carving, or scraping, as a form of rock art.

PICTOGRAPH: A symbolic pictorial image for a word, phrase, or idea that is painted or drawn on a surface with pigment.

PLEISTOCENE (KNOWN TO MANY AS THE *ICE AGE*): The geological era that lasted from about 11,700 to 2,580,000 years ago, spanning the earth's most recent period of colder climates where glaciers expanded.

PREHISTORY: The period of human history between the first uses of stone tools by hominins roughly 3.3 million years ago and the development of written languages and language systems.

TIMELINE

THIS VERY MOMENT: You are here, reading this book.

60 YEARS AGO: *Where the Wild Things Are* by Maurice Sendak is published in the United States.

83 YEARS AGO: Frida Kahlo paints *Self-Portrait with Thorn Necklace and Hummingbird* in Mexico.

148 YEARS AGO: Creation of the Statue of Liberty begins in France.

392 YEARS AGO: Taj Mahal is built in India.

600 YEARS AGO: Machu Picchu is constructed in Peru.

2,220 YEARS AGO: Terracotta Army is built for Qin Shi Huang's tomb in China.

4,500 YEARS AGO: Pyramids of Giza start to be constructed in Egypt.

4,600 YEARS AGO: Writing is developed in Sumer and Egypt, marking the beginning of "history" as recorded in writing.

6,000 YEARS AGO: Aboriginal "X-ray style" paintings created in shallow caves in Arnhem Land in northern Australia (see the cover of this book).

10,000 YEARS AGO: Many ice-age megafauna go extinct, including giant sloths.

11,600 YEARS AGO: Holocene begins, and conditions are optimal for human life to flourish.

17,000 YEARS AGO: Multiple human ancestors (*Homo sapiens*) work on Lascaux Caves over a period of time.

29,000 YEARS AGO: Oldest known use of ceramics in the form of figurines. (The "venus" or woman of Dolní Věstonice.)

40,000 YEARS AGO: Neanderthals go extinct.

70,000 YEARS AGO: Earliest example of abstract art or symbolic art from Blombos Cave, South Africa—stones engraved with grid or crosshatch patterns.

315,000 YEARS AGO: *Homo sapiens* enters the fossil record.

6 MILLION YEARS AGO: Humans diverge from closest ape relatives. Early hominins begin walking on two legs.

RESOURCES FOR FURTHER READING AND INVESTIGATION

Learn about all things rock art with Archaeology Podcast Network founder Chris Webster, archaeologist Dr. Alan Garfinkel, and a cast of expert guests:
ArcheoWebby and Rachel Roden. "A Podcast about Rock Art." *#Archpodnet*, June 26, 2020, https://www.archaeologypodcastnetwork.com/rockart.

Take a virtual 3D tour inside the Lascaux Caves:
Aujoulat, Norbert. "Visit the Cave." *Lascaux*, French Ministry of Culture, 2009, https://archeologie.culture.fr/lascaux/en/visit-cave.

Read a story inspired by the lone footprint left inside Cuevas de las manos:
Barron, T. A., and William Low. *Ghost Hands: A Story Inspired by Patagonia's Cave of the Hands.* New York: Philomel Books, 2011.

Explore an extensive catalog of rock art sites around the globe, rock art news, and archaeologists currently working in the field:
Robinson, Peter. *Bradshaw Foundation*, Bradshaw Foundation, 1992, https://www.bradshawfoundation.com/.

Dive deeper in into global rock art sites with engaging readings and photographs:
https://imagesdanslapierre.mcq.org/en/.

Visit a comprehensive online collection of rock art sites throughout the entire continent of Africa, compiled by TARA (Trust for African Rock Art):
https://africanrockart.org/.

Find out more about Aboriginal rock art, land, culture, and research in Australia:
https://rockartaustralia.org.au/.

IN MEMORY OF MY DAD,
STEPHEN D. SALYER.

With thanks to the Rock Art Network, Dr. Carolyn Boyd,
Dr. Janette Deacon, Noel Hidalgo Tan, Dr. Alan Garfinkel,
The Rock Art Podcast, Lindsay McAleavy, Ester Kwon,
and Maxim Elrod for their expertise and assistance.

ISBN 978-0-35-846984-1

The artist used ceramic sculpture, photography, colored pencil, charcoal,
pigment, and digital media to create the illustrations for this book.
Typography by Cara Llewellyn

22 23 24 25 26   RTLO   10 9 8 7 6 5 4 3 2 1

First Edition